ANIMAL ATTACK!

Hunting with MOUNTAIN LIONS

By Adeline Snyder

Gareth Stevens Publishing

Please visit our website, www.garethstevens.com. For a free color catalog of all our high-quality books, call toll free 1-800-542-2595 or fax 1-877-542-2596.

Library of Congress Cataloging-in-Publication Data

Snyder, Adeline.
Hunting with mountain lions / by Adeline Snyder.
p. cm. — (Animal attack!)
Includes index.
ISBN 978-1-4824-0517-0 (pbk.)
ISBN 978-1-4824-0522-4 (6-pack)
ISBN 978-1-4824-0516-3 (library binding)
1. Puma — Juvenile literature. I. Snyder, Adeline. II. Title.
QL737.C23 S649 2014
599.7524—dc23

First Edition

Published in 2014 by
Gareth Stevens Publishing
111 East 14th Street, Suite 349
New York, NY 10003

Designer: Katelyn E. Reynolds
Editor: Therese Shea

Photo credits: Cover, p. 1 (cover, pp. 1, 3–24 background image) Jason Edwards/National Geographic/Getty Images; cover, pp. 1, 3–24 (background graphic) pashabo/Shutterstock.com; cover, pp. 4–23 (splatter graphic) jgl247/Shutterstock.com; p. 5 Marci Renee/Shutterstock.com; p. 7 Thomas Kitchin & Victoria Hurst/All Canada Photos/Getty Images; pp. 8, 9, 18 iStockphoto/Thinkstock.com; p. 10 Daniel J. Cox/Stone/Getty Images; p. 11 Andy Rouse/StockImage/Getty Images; pp. 13, 14 Tom Brakefield/Stockbyte/Thinkstock.com; p. 15 Tom Brakefield/Photodisc/Getty Images; p. 17 Bruce Lichtenberger/Peter Arnold/Getty Images; p. 19 Purestock/Thinkstock.com; p. 21 Fuse/Thinkstock.com.

Printed in the United States of America

CPSIA compliance information: Batch #CW14GS: For further information contact Gareth Stevens, New York, New York at 1-800-542-2595.

CONTENTS

Words in the glossary appear in **bold** type the first time they are used in the text.

ON THE LOOKOUT

A large moose walks along the edge of the forest, stopping to eat grass as it goes. The sun is setting, and the forest is filled with dark shadows. The moose doesn't know something is watching it from above . . . until it's too late. A mountain lion leaps from a high branch and knocks the huge creature down.

The mountain lion's powerful **jaws** bite down. One bite is all it takes. The mountain lion has its dinner.

Fact Hunter

Mountain lions kill prey up to seven times their own weight.

Mountain lions like to stay hidden as they follow their prey.

COUGAR COUNTRY

Which is the most fearsome: a mountain lion, puma, cougar, or catamount? This is a trick question. These are all names for the same cat! They're called different names depending where they're found, and they live in many different places.

Mountain lion **habitats** can be found from Canada down through South America. In North America, they mostly live in the West, in areas where few people live and they can easily find prey. Their prey includes moose, deer, coyotes, beavers, rabbits, birds, fish, skunks, and squirrels.

Fact Hunter

A small population of mountain lions called Florida panthers lives in the forests and **swamps** of that state.

The Florida panther is **endangered**, with fewer than 100 left.

HABITATS

Mountain lions are found in forests, plains, swamps, deserts, and mountains. They choose habitats with places they can hide so they can sneak up on their prey.

Mountain lions like to live alone. They stay in their territory, which can be large if there isn't a lot of food or smaller if there is plenty. These big cats only meet other mountain lions to fight over land or to **mate**. They mark their territory with scratches and **scents** to tell other cats it's taken!

This mountain lion is marking its territory by scratching the bark of a tree.

A HUNTER'S BODY

Mountain lions are built for hunting. They have large paws for holding down prey. They have sharp claws for grabbing on to animals. Their powerful back legs make them excellent jumpers.

Mountain lions also have a backbone that bends as they move. That means they can change direction easily as they're darting between trees or following prey that's trying to get away. They can run as fast as 50 miles (80 km) per hour!

Fact Hunter

Mountain lions can jump as far as 40 feet (12.2 m)!

A mountain lion's strength and speed make it a predator to fear.

LOOK BEHIND YOU!

Even though mountain lions are so fast and powerful, they're often sneaky! They hunt alone and often at night so they can use the darkness to hide. Their large paws have padding that helps them move very quietly.

Mountain lions like to surprise their prey. They may jump down from a tree branch or follow closely behind an animal and then **pounce**. A mountain lion's bite is so strong that a single bite may be all it takes to break an animal's neck.

Fact Hunter

Mountain lions can eat porcupines, quills and all!

This mountain lion is about to catch its next meal.

WHAT A DRAG

A mountain lion might eat 20 pounds (9 kg) of meat at a time. So, if a mountain lion kills large prey, such as a deer, it might not eat it all right away. Instead, the big cat may drag it to a different place and cover it with leaves or grass, or even bury it.

That way, the mountain lion can keep its big meal away from other animals. It can come back to feed when it wants to.

Fact Hunter

A mountain lion may kill a large animal once every 10 to 14 days.

Mountain lions don't like water, but that doesn't stop this mountain lion from following a deer!

DENS AND CUBS

Mountain lions have dens, but they move often within their territory. They mostly use the dens as places to shelter from weather or to have cubs.

Mother mountain lions usually have three or four cubs at a time. Every few weeks, she'll move her family. She doesn't want other male mountain lions to find them. They might kill them! The cubs hide in the den until they're ready to hunt. This is when they're about 6 months old.

Fact Hunter

Mountain lion cubs have spots and rings on their tails.

Mountain lion cubs are also called kittens.

ATTACKING PEOPLE

Perhaps the scariest thing about mountain lions is that they've been known to attack people! Mountain lions usually try to avoid people. However, people are sometimes attacked while walking alone through forests and other mountain lion habitats. Mountain lions may mistake them for prey.

It's actually better not to run when faced with a mountain lion. Park rangers suggest making a lot of noise, throwing rocks and sticks, and trying to fight back—this is something mountain lions' prey wouldn't do!

When entering a wooded area, be alert and pay attention to signs about wildlife.

HUNTER AND HUNTED

Because mountain lions have been known to harm people, people attacked them. People shot, trapped, and poisoned mountain lions to keep them off their lands. Part of the problem is that people have moved closer or even into mountain lion habitats and territory. So, the big cats look for prey in this area.

Mountain lions are important for keeping the populations of other animals in check. They need land where they can roam freely and play their role in their habitats.

Mountain Lions by the Numbers

length	5 to 8 feet (1.5 to 2.4 m), from nose to tip of tail
height	about 3 feet (0.9 m), at shoulder
weight	up to 200 pounds (91 kg)
life span	about 12 years in the wild
population	about 30,000

GLOSSARY

endangered: in danger of dying out

habitat: the natural place where an animal or plant lives

jaw: one of the bones that hold the teeth and make up the mouth

mate: one of two animals that come together to make babies. Also, to come together to make babies.

pounce: to jump suddenly toward or on something

scent: a smell

swamp: an area with trees that is covered with water at least part of the time

FOR MORE INFORMATION

Books

Bradley, James V. *The Mountain Lion*. New York, NY: Chelsea Clubhouse, 2006.

Hamilton, Sue. *Ambushed by a Cougar*. Edina, MN: ABDO Publishing, 2010.

Somervill, Barbara A. *Florida Panther*. Ann Arbor, MI: Cherry Lake Publishing, 2009.

Websites

Fact Sheet: Mountain Lions
www.defenders.org/mountain-lion/basic-facts
Read about this amazing big cat and how some people are trying to help them.

Florida Panther
www.nwf.org/wildlife/wildlife-library/mammals/florida-panther.aspx
Find out more about the endangered Florida panther.

Mountain Lion (Puma, Cougar)
www.sandiegozoo.org/animalbytes/t-puma.html
Check out some fun facts about these fearsome predators.

Publisher's note to educators and parents: Our editors have carefully reviewed these websites to ensure that they are suitable for students. Many websites change frequently, however, and we cannot guarantee that a site's future contents will continue to meet our high standards of quality and educational value. Be advised that students should be closely supervised whenever they access the Internet.

INDEX